on the scenic route

on the scenic route

roam the haiku poem heart
appreciation

Steve Meleney

A dedication:
to countless friends and friendships
open and engaged

Steve Meleney's journey began on the bustling east coast of the United States, where he grew up as the fourth of five siblings. Little did he know that a summer vacation to Denver at the age of twenty would turn into a lifelong adventure spanning over fifty years in the Mile-High City and the picturesque landscapes of Colorado.

In the heart of this journey, he crossed paths with his wife, Yuko, a native of Niigata, Japan. Their love story has unfolded for over thirty years, bringing together cultures and creating a beautiful tapestry of shared experiences. As an independent contractor courier navigating the roads of the Front Range for over three decades, Steve has become intimately acquainted with the scenic wonders that surround him.

The spark of haiku ignited in Steve twenty-three years ago as he prepared for a memorable trip to Japan with Yuko and his mother. Folding origami cranes and composing 5-7-5 syllable poems, Steve found a new passion that would weave its way through the fabric of his life. The ensuing Springtime journey of 2000 was filled with heartwarming moments that fueled his creative spirit, and he continued to pen haiku-style poems.

A pivotal moment unfolded during a Christmas holiday at his mother's home. An outing to the movies with family sparked the creation of a haiku that, unexpectedly, led his mother to share a treasure trove of poems she had written in her school days and kept in a secret journal for seventy years. This revelation became a heartfelt breakthrough for the entire family.

In the years that followed, Steve's haiku became snapshots of inspiration and heartfelt experiences, shared through greeting cards and social media as a delightful hobby.

You are invited and encouraged to engage your own inherent and ever youthful vigor and creativity.

Open the door to your fresh possibility:

on the scenic route
roam the haiku poem heart
appreciation

Please enjoy!

most wonderful mom
poetry of youth journal
warm heart strength reveal

engage

engage the battle
to explore inherent heart
remaining fearless

praise

heart continuous
songs of unending praise flow
in vital rhythm

radiate

essential embrace
radiate regal light smiles
dancing cheerfully

pauses to refresh
treasure stillness eternal
soaring on at ease

stir

rooted in good friends
prevailing Spring breezes stir
breakthrough of the heart

penetrate

single-minded shine
thoroughly encouraging
penetrate the heart

conviction

aiming to open
ripe condition of the heart
sail with conviction

spark

spark a beginning
to empower fresh ascent
up trailheads of gold

create

create the mission
to revive hope full spirits
on the scenic route

summon

mountain of courage
roaring from the heart summon
emancipation

inspire

cheerful in earnest
young heart of challenge inspire
abiding vigor

thanks

thanks a thousand times
instantly reduce the gaps
re-opening heart

grasp

joyfully engaged
grasp the chalice of being
ready to start fresh

offer

haiku for Yuko
ever in the key of Spring
offer from the heart

shine

lion of the heart
shine extraordinary light
beyond the limits

celebrate

celebrate immense
heart of the thrilling journey
at a full gallop

imbue

one sonorous heart
imbue light vitality
with sparkling eyes

dance

onward robustly
glorious cherry blossoms
dance the enduring

courageous

marshal courageous
praise as a creative force
on the scenic route

dignity

from heart dignity
all things hold deeper meaning
vast and radiant

significant

heart significant
tall and firm in the maelstrom
indestructible

gratitude

bow of gratitude
for the arduous journey
far reaches dig deep

imagine

vast creative heart
this is the imagine year
fulfill the promise

emerge

after sleepless night
from closely held heart secrets
emerge triumphant

open

embracing the bright
youthful sun relentlessly
open the way next

align

heart of Spring align
river flow of good fortune
fill up an ocean

impart

joy in dialogue
impart the strength to triumph
forward intrepid

widen

time flies bubbles rise
open these arriving eyes
widen to the skies

capture

in the heart moment
capture exalted essence
on the scenic route

attain

heart deepening faith
attain eternal fine health
no separation

triumph

triumph over doubt
scaling a majestic heart
inside tranquil bright

mirrors reflect back
clearly composed creation
to invigorate

greet

cheering in mid-air
greet the inexhaustible
possibility

stimulate

fragrant renaissance
stimulate without limit
through the nurturing

door

this door promises
to open limitless sky
opportunity

show

show young visitors
journeying from the future
serene victory

explore

into the unknown
explore rebirth of the heart
feeling expansive

ignite

starburst of courage
ignite compassionate heart
throughout the cosmos

smile

smile positive light
exploring heart potential
on the scenic route

roar

intentionally
each day being the present
roar vigorously

refresh

vitally refresh
oceans of heart awaken
re-discovery

lift

stand with confidence
bathing in elevated light
to lift a young heart

forge

treasure at the core
precious youthfulness itself
forge the cherished dream

with care together
weave a durable fabric
for the long travel

seed

each kaleidoscope
bouquet of perennials
seed to replenish

empower

rhythmic harmony
empower the will to live
in activation

raise

light flurries of snow
ever floating in the air
raise spirits as one

fortune

anticipating
open the fortune cookie
on the scenic route

soar

a boundless sunrise
soar with the engaging wind
to the horizon

gather

assiduously
gather fine ingredients
for the Spring of heart

illuminate

another candle
illuminate the landscape
with quiet gusto

Milton Keynes UK
Ingram Content Group UK Ltd.
UKRC031356260324
440150UK00006B/74

9798218397234